SWINGING MAD

Edited by
Albert B. Feldstein

WARNER BOOKS

A Warner Communications Company

WARNER BOOKS EDITION

Copyright © 1970, 1971 and 1977
by E.C. Publications, Inc.

All rights reserved.
No part of this book may be reproduced without permission.
For information address E.C. Publications, Inc., 485 Madison
Ave., New York, N.Y. 10022.

ISBN 0-446-86352-1

**Title "MAD" used with permission of its owner,
E.C. Publications, Inc.**

This Warner Books Edition is published by
arrangement with E.C. Publications, Inc.

Designed by Thomas Nozkowski

Warner Books, Inc., 75 Rockefeller Plaza, New York, N.Y. 10019

 A Warner Communications Company

Printed in the United States of America

Not associated with Warner Press, Inc. of Anderson, Indiana

First Printing: October, 1977

10 9 8 7 6 5 4 3 2 1

FORCED-FEDS DEPT.

From time to time, the F.B.I. has been severely criticized for the way it handles its affairs. However, in the series presented each week on television, the F.B.I. is depicted as handling matters in a way that would hardly even raise an eyebrow. Which is why we call our version of this show

THE

F.I.B.*

* Editor's Note: One of the sponsors of this weekly TV series is a leading automobile manufacturer. From the subtle references and plugs they make throughout the show, see if you can guess which one.

ARTIST: ANGELO TORRES

WRITER: DICK DE BARTOLO

"On October 19th, a man posing as wastepaper basket repairman gained access to the vault of the Last National Bank . . .

"He escaped from the scene of his crime in a sleek-looking Ford Mustang equipped with bucket seats and stick shift . . .

Torres

"The FIB was called in on the case because among the items missing from the vault were Federal Securities, Government Bonds, and a bunch of Mr. J. Edgar Hoover's trading stamps!

"FIB Inspector Lucas Oilyskin, along with Special Agent Tame Coldly and Special Guest Agent L.T.D. Thunderbird, following a few slim clues and several fat hunches, found the hide-out of the safe-cracker, who had returned to the scene of the crime and was living in the bank vault . . .

"The safe-cracker was apprehended, and also caught, and sentenced to 99 years in prison. However, his sentence was reduced to 6 months for having the good taste to use a Mustang as the get-away car. The case was closed and—"

Hold it! HOLD IT!! That blabbermouth Narrator has gone **too far!** I don't mind that every week he tells **most** of the story . . . but this time, he's told the **whole thing!!** We're two minutes into the show, and already he's through the **Epilog! Now** . . . can we please start again with **another** story!? And if that Narrator tells too much **THIS** time, I'll have him arrested for possessing an **illegal mouth!**

On December 17th, a young woman came into the Washington, D.C., Office and lodged a complaint that her boyfriend had run off with her diamonds. She was told th*mph—phmmmph* . . ."

Okay! **We'll** take it from here!

Sorry, Miss! Unless it's an inter-State crime, the FIB can not intercede! Do you know what State your boyfriend is in **now?**

I magine he's in a state of ecstasy! Those diamonds were worth a fortune!

Then he's **crossed State lines! We'll** take the **case!** Inspector Oilyskin! Would you come in here, please?

"And so, 'Sweetheart' was caught, convicted and sent to prison for 40 years! Jackie Paxton got her jewels back! And the men of the FIB went on to another case! This case involved an underworld counterfeit ring run by a man named Sidney Gwir—"

ONE DAY IN A BUS DEPOT

BZZOWNT!

ACE VENDING COMPANY
5721 WEST AVENUE
Room 314

Recently, someone published a book called "Children's Letters To God." It was so popular, another book was published called "More Children's Letters To God." Now, that one is so popular, by the time you read this article, they'll probably publish one called "Still More Children's Letters To God." Well, it seems to us that there's an awful lot of one-way letter-writing going on, so MAD remedies the situation with

Answers To Children's Letters

–From GOD

WRITERS: DICK DeBARTOLO & DONALD K. EPSTEIN

Dear Mary,
My notes about your
behavior are written
in the Big Book in
<u>indelible</u> ink. But
thank you anyway for
the nice eraser.
                    Love,

                    —God—

Dear Jerry,
I do spend a lot of time in
Brooklyn, but that was not
Me you saw on the IND subway
last Saturday afternoon.

                    Love,

                    —God—

Dear Lisa,
Your forthcoming trip to California
sounds very exciting. I would love
to see you, too, but TWA does not
stop here on the way to Los Angeles.
                    Fondly,

                    —God—

Dear Tommy,
The reason you cannot find me
in the telephone book is that
my number is unlisted.

Best wishes,

—god—

Dear Beth,
I am sorry, but it is
not up to me to make
bacon "kosher."

Sincerely,

god

Dear Bruce,
I am sorry it rained last Sunday
when you were supposed to have
your Boy Scout Hike, but I
cannot send you a copy of my
"Guaranteed Long-Range Forecast"
to avoid disappointments like
that in the future.

Faithfully yours,

—god—

Dear Laurie,
Yes, I am watching you all
the time. But that is no
excuse for not taking a bath.
Love,

God

Dear Sharon,
I was very pleased to learn
that you think of your good
deeds as "deposits in the
Bank of Life." However, I
do not have the facilities
for sending you a regular
monthly statement.

Best regards,

God

Dear Leslie,
Thank you for your concern,
but I do not find it a
"drag" working Sundays and
religious holidays.

Sincerely,

God

Dear Robin,
Even though your daddy
says they are "God-awful,"
I am not responsible for
the shows you watch on
television.

Sincerely,

Dear Susie,
I know you have doubts
about my existence, but
in the future please
do not address your
letters to:

Occupant,
Heaven,
U.S.A.
Thank you.

Sincerely,

Dear Randy and Ricky,
It does not matter
which one of you
sleeps where. I'm
just as close to
the one in the
bottom bunk.

Love,

Dear Edward,
You sound like a very enter-
prising young man, but I
really do not feel that there
is a market for holy water in
"No-deposit, No-return Bottles."
                    Sincerely,

                    —God—

Dear Jonathan,
Thanks for your inquiry, but I
really do not have a favorite.
I like all the Commandments.
                    Love,

                    —God—

Dear Linda,
I am glad you received
a new camera for your
birthday, but it would
be against the rules
to let you come up here
and take pictures.
                    Love,

                    —God—

Dear Tracy,
You may tell your mommy
I said it is <u>not</u> a "sin"
to leave the peas in
your TV dinner.

                    Love,

Dear Harvey,
Yes, I can hear you
singing in the church
choir every Sunday.

Do not call Us --
We will call you.
                Sincerely,

THE LIGHTER SIDE OF...

SOUND EQUIP

ARTIST & WRITER: DAVE BERG

You're always tinkering with that **Hi-Fi** set-up of yours! From the minute you walk in the door until you go to bed, it's noise . . . noise . . . **NOISE!**

You never have a **kind word** for me anymore! You never take me **out** anymore! All you do, night after night, is fool with that—**THING!!**

Kilimanjaro!!!

MENT

What **is** it? **Tell** me! What's so **fascinating** about a radio that you prefer it to me?!

I can **turn it off** when I want to!

Oh, my goodness! What happened to you?!

I . . . I just took a **terrible beating!** I—I was **completely surrounded** by **FOUR** of them! Two were hitting me from the **front**, and two from the **rear!**

Four big hoodlums?!

No . . . four big **LOUDSPEAKERS!!**

That's not a radio!

That's a whiskey flask!

Our **son** just demonstrated the new **stereo tape player** he installed in his **car!**

BV190

That son of ours left his big, complicated **Hi-Fi** set on! I want to shut it **off**—but look at all the **knobs** and **switches**! How in heck do you **do** it??

Hah! Listen to the big leading member of the **Women's Lib Movement** asking her male chauvinist husband how to handle **electronic equipment**!

Your **mouth** may be going all the time, demanding equality with men—but, as you can see, you're **not** our equals when it comes to **technology** or **complicated machinery**!

Admit you're inferior in many areas, and I'll show you how **simple** it is!

Okay! **Okay!** I'm an **inferior female!** Now—show me how to shut the darn thing off!!

You pull out the plug!

Hey, I see you have one of those new Digital AM - FM Alarm Clocks! How does it work?

First I check with the phone company to see if my digits are correct! Then, I switch this knob to AM or FM! Then I tune in a station with this knob . . .

Then, with this knob, I set the time I want to awake! And with this knob, I set it for either "radio" or "alarm"! This knob keeps the radio playing until I fall asleep! And this knob controls the time it will play until it shuts itself off!

Sounds like a great way to wake up in the morning!

It's also a great way to put myself to sleep at night!

You mean because it lulls you into dreamland with soft music?!

No, I mean by the time I'm finished setting the whole thing up, I'm totally exhausted!!

HAROLD! DINNER'S ON THE TABLE!

Save your **breath**, Mom! Dad can't **hear** you!

He **can't?!** Why **not?**

He's locked in the den, listening to the "Brad Crandall Phone-In Show" with his **earphones** on!

That means he can't hear **ANY** outside noises! So there's absolutely **no way** to **communicate** with him!

Really? Well, I'm not **licked yet!**

Hello . . . Brad Crandall? Will you please tell my husband, Harold, that his **dinner** is on the table!

I didn't know the Groom was hard of hearing!

He's NOT! . . . Oh, you mean that thing in his ear? Steve is a baseball nut! There's a transistor radio in his pocket, and he's actually listening to the ball game while he's greeting people on the receiving line!

I want to wish you both all the happiness in the world . . .

Thank you!

This must be the happiest day of your life!

Oh, it is!

BELIEVE ME, it is!

THE METS JUST WON!!

ONE
DAY
IN
A
PET
SHOP

There's a revolution going on and it's not being fought in the jungles of Asia or the mountains of South America. It's being fought in college dormitories, ski lodges, motels, summer resorts, drive-in movies and in homes all over America. In case you're out of it, we're talking about the Sexual Revolution. Let us, therefore, salute the valiant fighters in this intimate struggle as we here at MAD — yes, MAD — present . . .

GREETING CARDS

FOR

THE

SEXUAL

REVOLUTION

ARTIST: BOB CLARKE   WRITER: FRANK JACOBS

To An Obscene Phone Caller

At ten o'clock in your hometown
Some phone begins to ring;
And when the party picks it up
You do your lurid thing;
You murmur your obscenities
With lewd, salacious glee;
With all the smut on sale today,
How nice to get you free!

To
A
Reluctant Female

With sex so big, it's time that we
    Both joined the revolution;
And yet, my pet, you still refuse
    To make a contribution;
Let's hope one day some sign of lust
    Within your heart appears;
I only bring it up 'cause we've
    Been wed for seven years!

To A
Producer Of Skin Flicks

Each picture that you make is like
A sexual excursion—
With mixed-up nymphos, orgies
And a plot of sick perversion;

You should get wise that folks today
Don't think your films are groovy;
With sex in real-life like it is,
Who needs a dirty movie?

To A Gay Liberationist

Down city streets throughout the land
  You're marching by the score;
And though you're screaming for your rights
  It's all a crashing bore;
You shout that you are victimized
  By bigoted attacks;
Forgive us if we're more concerned
  With Indians and Blacks!

To A

Make-Out Artist

You swing with every chick you meet;
 You're just a sex-mad creature;
This week you've had a stewardess,
 Three stenos and a teacher;
On every date you've always got
 A brand-new girl in hand;
Perhaps it's 'cause one night with you
 Is all that they can stand!

To A Sex Fetishist

You wear long boots with pointed heels—
 They're good for getting kicks;
Your rumpus room is full of whips—
 They're great for swinging chicks;

Your weirdo chums wear leather gear
 And chain you to a chair;
What fun to have a hobby that
 Your friends and you can share!

To A Very Special Girl

No other chick can match you, kid,
  For sensual desire;
Like, wow, you really know the ways
  To set a guy on fire;
In gratitude for all those nights
  This card is sent with joy
From Marvin, Danny, Harold, Bill,
  Sylvester, Fred and Roy!

To A Recent Conquest

I can't forget that date of ours
  When passions were inflamed;
You bit, you clawed, you turned into
  A savage beast, untamed;
Although the moment that we shared
  Was frantic, fierce and thrilling;
I wonder how it might have been
  If, sweetheart, you'd been willing!

To A First Love

You cry out with the lust of youth
  And, sweetheart, so do I;
The heartfelt yearnings that we feel
  We simply can't deny;
And yet, despite the joy we seek,
  We know that we must wait;
Perhaps next year we'll make the scene
  When both of us turn eight!

To An Ancient Lover

Your years now number 85,
    And yet you spend your time
Impressing girls one-fourth your age
    That you're still in your prime;
Although it's true you always fail,
    You still should take a bow;
You've got the will; it's simply that
    You can't remember how!

ONE EVENING IN A BATHTUB

THAT'LL BE THE DAY!

ARTIST:
PAUL COKER, JR.

WRITER:
DICK DE BARTOLO

You Know

OVER

You Know It's REALLY OVER When . . .

. . . he asks you to return his books you borrowed, even though you're not through reading them.

ARTIST: JACK RICKARD

WRITERS: AL JAFFEE & GLORIA L. RICH

It's REALLY When...

You Know It's REALLY OVER When . . .

. . . he drives you home after a date
and leaves the motor running!

You Know It's REALLY OVER When . . .

. . . he offers to drive the gang home, and you're the first one he drops off!

You Know It's REALLY OVER When . . .

. . . he starts talking about kissing and sex from a hygienic point of view!

You Know It's REALLY OVER When . . .

. . . you discover he's gotten an unlisted number, and he neglected to tell you about it.

You Know It's REALLY OVER When . . .

. . . he only dances the fast numbers with you, and sits out the slow romantic ones!

You Know It's REALLY OVER When . . .

. . . he says, "We can't go on meeting like this!" . . . and you're both single!

You Know It's REALLY OVER When . . .

. . . you notice that, lately, whenever you're out together, he yawns a lot and looks at his watch!

You Know It's REALLY OVER When . . .

. . . the house is yours, the lights are low, the music is groovy . . . and he spends the night playing with Fido!

You Know It's REALLY OVER When . . .

. . . she suddenly announces she has "just the right girl for you!"

You Know It's REALLY OVER When . . .

. . . you hear giggling, whispering and slurping noises as she breaks your date because of a headache!

You Know It's REALLY OVER When . . .

. . . you notice the garbage collector wearing the scarf you spent six months knitting for "him"!

You Know It's REALLY OVER When . . .

. . . she starts introducing you to people as one of her "oldest and dearest friends!"

You Know It's REALLY OVER When . . .

. . . the song you've always considered "our song" comes on the radio, and he snaps it off, saying, "I've always hated that thing!"

You Know It's REALLY OVER When . . .

. . . you call him up, and "she" answers!

You Know It's REALLY OVER When . . .

. . . you start noticing how, lately, someone is always dropping in just when you think you're going to spend an evening alone in her pad.

You Know It's REALLY OVER When . . .

. . . you go to the movies, and he no longer cares about finding "two together"!

You Know It's REALLY OVER When . . .

. . . he takes you to a "McDonald's" on the anniversary of your first date.

You Know It's REALLY OVER When . . .

. . . his recent letters end with "Very truly yours,"!

You Know It's REALLY OVER When . . .

. . . he's no longer interested in your root canal work!

You Know It's REALLY OVER When . . .

. . . she tells you that no matter what happens, she'd like to always have you as a friend!

It figures! When man becomes confused at the irrationality of the world around him, he looks for meaning, purpose and reason in areas that are often more confusing than the irrationality of the world around him. Don't bother to figure that one out, just read MAD's version of a magazine dedicated to mysticism, and the "Gypsy'" in all of us . . .

INCREDIBLE OCCULT MAGAZINE

DECEMBER
1923, 1971, 1989

50c
Cross Our
Palm With
SILVER

Combining Astral Digest, Ectoplasm Age,
and The Saturday Evening Post

The Reincarnation Of
CHARLES DICKENS
Picks Up Our Garbage

☆ ☆ ☆

How The 1965
Venus-Neptune
Conjunction
Ruined My Son's
Bar Mitzvah

☆ ☆ ☆

Palmistry And YOU:

Does Suicide Affect
The Lifeline?

☆ ☆ ☆

My Life As A
Smith-Corona Portable
In Nutley, New Jersey

☆ ☆ ☆

Poltergeists Make
Lousy Lovers

☆ ☆ ☆

Do The Ancients
Communicate With Us
Through Ed Sullivan?

☆ ☆ ☆

How I Drove My
Power Mower To
Anchorage, Alaska
In A Post-Hypnotic
Trance

ARTIST: GEORGE WOODBRIDGE   WRITER: FRANK JACOBS

ASK OMAR THE ASTROLOGER

Dear Omar:
I am a professor of astrophysics at M.I.T. and for 16 years have studied astrology from every aspect. I have concluded that there is absolutely no scientific basis for belief in the movements of the stars and planets.

T.S.
Boston, Mass.

Dear T.S.
Such hare-brained views can seriously mar the efforts of dedicated occultists. The editors of this magazine join me in urging our readers to pay no attention to fuzzy-minded intellectual nuts like yourself. If M.I.T. wasn't a Libra, I'd really fix your wagon!

Dear Omar:
I am a Virgo who is thinking of taking a walk around the block. I never do anything without first checking it out on my chart, but I see no mention of strolling. When is the best time for me to undertake such a venture?

J.D.
Jersey City, N.J.

Dear J.D.
This, of course, depends upon the opposition of Jupiter to Venus. As of last week, they still weren't speaking, so I'm afraid that my answer must be an unqualified "Maybe."

Dear Omar:
Is it true that two people born under the same sign share similar personalities, beliefs, and outlooks?

A.B.F.
Candlewood Lake, Conn.

Dear A.B.F.
Yes, absolutely. The following chart will show the marked similarities found in people born under the same sign . . .

AQUARIUS	
William Tecumseh Sherman (Jan. 21)	"Stonewall" Jackson (Feb. 8)
PISCES	
Liz Taylor (Feb. 27)	Pat Nixon (Feb. 9)
AIRES	
Eugene McCarthy (March 29)	Gen. William Westmoreland (March 26)
TAURUS	
Dr. Spock (May 2)	Mayor Daley (May 15)
GEMINI	
Guy Lombardo (June 19)	Paul McCartney (June 18)
CANCER	
Phyllis Diller (July 17)	Gina Lollobrigida (July 4)
LEO	
George Bernard Shaw (July 26)	Casey Stengel (July 30)
VIRGO	
Sophia Loren (Sept. 20)	Twiggy (Sept. 19)
LIBRA	
Truman Capote (Sept. 30)	Mickey Mantle (Oct. 20)
SCORPIO	
Chiang kai-Shek (Oct. 31)	Mao tse-Tung (Nov. 19)
SAGITTARIUS	
William F. Buckley (Nov. 24)	Abbie Hoffman (Nov. 30)
CAPRICORN	
Joan Baez (Jan. 9)	Barry Goldwater (Jan. 1)

Dear Omar:
According to my horoscope, the entrance of Neptune into Capricorn last year meant it was a good time for investment.

So I poured my life savings into an oil stock which turned out to be phony and I lost every penny, not to mention my car and house. How do you explain this?

N.M.
Wurtsboro, N.Y.

Dear N.M.
Oh, that rascal Neptune! How this naughty planet loves a practical joke!

Don't worry, N.M., Neptune always evens things out, and will probably make it up to you when it enters Capricorn next trip around in 2134!

Dear Omar:
I am a Gemini with Uranus in my ninth house, Mercury in my fourth house, and Mars in my first house. What shall I do?

A.K.
Encino, Cal.

Dear A.K.
Move into an apartment.

Pick up these latest
SOUND WAVES
from
SEANCE RECORDS

WARREN G. HARDING
Sings the Songs of
BURT BACHARACH

JULIUS CAESAR

The Complete Play
Enacted By The
ORIGINAL CAST

That Incredible Year
4283 B.C.

The SOUNDS, The GRUNTS,
The EXCITEMENT of That
Wonderful Bygone Era!

On sale now at your local
Occult
Record Center

The Marquis de Sade Lived In My Body!

An *Incredible Occult* True-Life Experience
by Morton Fenster

It all started out as a regular seance that night back in 1968. Already we'd chatted with the spirits of Paul Revere, Woodrow Wilson, and Harvey Schmeer, a lately deceased third cousin of mine in Denver who'd died owing me twenty-three dollars. Then, suddenly, a chill swept across the room. The table turned sideways in mid-air, and I knew at that moment that the MARQUIS DE SADE WAS RIGHT THERE IN THE ROOM WITH US! I could feel his powerful presence getting stronger and stronger until at last his murky, menacing spirit closed in and TOOK OVER MY BODY! The women screamed! The men gasped! I belched! There was no doubt about it—*I had become the Marquis de Sade!* Without warning, I was seized by dark, sinister passions. I embarked on a wild, violent reign of unbridled lust and weird, unnatural cravings. I ran the gamut of sexual fetishes, sensual perversions, deviated septums, and other degenerate pastimes too lurid to think about, let alone list!

For six incredible hours it lasted—my will yielding in every lascivious way to his every sadistic pleasure. I struggled to break free, and finally rallied the forces of my own strong moral fiber and righteous indignation to scream:

"Go away, Marquis! GO AWAY!"

And suddenly, as quickly as he came, he was gone. I was possessed no more! I was no longer the Marquis de Sade; I was Morton Fenster! No longer a creature of lust craving every carnal pleasure; but a balding tax accountant living with my wife and three kids in Muncie, Indiana. And suddenly I found myself screaming:

"Come back, Marquis! COME BACK!"

But it was too late. The Marquis had *(Cont. on page 57)*

the occult grapevine

Mystic Meanderings for the Cosmic Community by Claire Voyant

It's all over with Jomar and Zelda Mishkin (she's the medium). Seems Jomar didn't approve of the week-end Zelda spent in Cleveland with Benjamin Franklin (that D.O.M.) . . . A hearty "Welcome back" to Pittsburgh mystic Brahma Bregstein who's home after spending a well-earned vacation visiting friends in 1981 . . . Vibrate your cosmic condolences to these ill-starred occultists: To karma victim Mauve Muncrief, an Aquarius-Pisces cusp who lost her court battle to legally change her sign; and to Automatic-Writing Wizard Lance Wickwire, who is serving two years in prison for writing John Paul Getty's name on checks while in a trance.

* * * *

After feuding for fifteen years, rival occultists Orion O'Ryan (left) and Booker Bokar flipped a coin to settle once and for all who was the true reincarnation of Napoleon. Bokar lost and is now seeking the cosmic rights to Alexander the Great.

A tip of the psychic hat to super-seer Joshua Freen for correctly predicting the date of his rebirth . . . Numerologists Eric Omicron and Seth Sholtar are still exchanging death curses. The feud flared up when Seth accused Eric of trying to 18

his 46 . . . **Baltimore occultists are giving the cold-shoulder treatment to Tea-Leaf Reader Phaedra Dinwiddie. Seems she undercharged a customer, then compounded her goof by predicting a piece of bad news . . . Lincoln, Nebraska's own Abner Meerchaum has become the first Earthling to ride in the new "Jumbo" flying saucer. "There's a lot more room," says Meerchaum, "and it gets you to Orion in half the time despite the fact that we had to circle Betelguese Airport for more than a lightyear."**

WHERE ARE THEY NOW DEPT: Cassiopeia Waxrush, first mystic to prove that hamsters meditate, is now a Rosicrucian recruiter in Milwaukee . . . Draco Donnelly, who 20 years ago discovered William Shakespeare's ghost in a Kansas City Super-market, is now a door-to-door mandala-mender in Santa Barbara . . . Capella Calhoun, the former Miss Demon-Worship of 1949, runs a boarding house for retired apparitions in West Orange, N.J.

* * * *

Sorcerer Presto Pollack has moved back in with his wife after a 6 month separation. Presto solved his domestic problems by turning his mother-in-law into a Beagle.

BIRTH NOTES: It's a boy for Madam Myra the Medium. The father is most likely Jacques Casanova . . . It's a future automobile salesman who'll marry an airline stewardess and settle down in Altoona for prophet Lee Lumbar and his lovely wife Lulu.

* * * *

Occult insiders expect Vulcan Freen to walk off with the "Sorcerer-of-the-Year" Award. Vulcan won plaudits for his recent conjuring in a New York City restaurant when he actually made a waiter materialize . . . LOOK ALIKES DEPT: Quandra Muldoon, authoress of "How To Win At Tarot Cards," and Satan.

* * * *

HOW ABOUT THAT? DEPT: During the recent favorable Venus-Saturn conjunction, Astrologer Mandrake Meerschaum was wiped out in the stock market, broke both legs in a Yoga experiment, and lost his home in a four-alarm fire. Undaunted, Mandrake will sue the Solar System.

INCREDIBLE

OCCULT

CLASSIFIED ADS

FOR SALE

Slightly used crystal ball. Barely gazed at. Used only for an hour each Sunday by a 78-year-old widow schoolteacher to talk to her departed husband. Best offer takes. Box 703

PERSONAL

Want to talk with God? Call Me collect. (819) 993-4909

Okay, Brutus! I know you're reincarnated out there somewhere! Be a man for once and let's have it out—just you and me! Don't bring your friends! Write to me: J. Caesar, c/o Schwartz, 41 Elm, Oakville, Kansas

Milton, my only begotten son. Mars is in Libra, Saturn is in Pisces, and you still want to marry that fortune-hunting slut from Dallas! Heed the stars before I have a heart attack! And wear your galoshes. Mother

I am the reincarnation of Hokar, the 12th High Priestess of the Fallons, a civilization vanished into the Indian Ocean. I would like to meet a nice Albuquerque dentist. Box 252

WANTED TO TRADE

Will swap a 12th century Ethiopian poltergeist with a sinus condition for two decks of Tarot cards. Box 5

FOR RENT

Will supply sleep-in apparitions, poltergeists, etc., for haunting. Send for list of satisfied customers, rate scale, particulars. Apparitions Unlimited, Box 32

GUIDANCE SOUGHT

Would appreciate some occultist telling me why my Ouija board spells only four-letter words. Philip Roth, Box 96

BLACK MAGIC

Possessed by Demons? Plagued by Evil Spirits? You need CURSE-OFF, the new miracle curse remover in the aerosol can. Fight old curses the modern way for only $4.98. CURSE-OFF, Box 13, Wingbat, Ohio

Pestered by obnoxious neighbors? A mean boss? A nagging wife? You need CURSE-ON, the new miracle curse invoker in the aerosol can. Apply new curses the modern way for only $4.98. CURSE-ON, Box 711, Wingbat, Ohio

You are reading this ad. You are absorbing its meaning. You are putting a ten-dollar bill in an envelope and mailing it to Zarkov the Hypnotist, Box 414.

FREE!
A LIFE-SIZE REPLICA OF
AN ALBINO WARLOCK'S
DENTURE

When You Join The

Cult-Of-The-Month Club

Now you can share the Mystic Experiences of the Newest Religious Cults RIGHT IN YOUR OWN HOME! Each month you will receive appropriate amulets, robes, incantations, pledges, bat tongues, candles, stag films, incense—everything you need to participate in the secret RITES of the Club's MONTHLY OFFERING!

**HERE IS
A PREVIEW OF
THE FABULOUS
CULTS TO COME...**

THE SEVENTH CHURCH OF OOG

Headquartered in an abandoned comfort station in beautiful downtown Fresno, The CHURCH OF OOG believes in the divinity of the earlobe. Members meditate alternate Thursdays wearing see-through shrouds of luminous Mediterranean algae.

THE VIBRATORY SYNOD

These cultists have uncovered a set of Atlantean stone obelisks which give off vibrations corresponding to each member's Zip Code number. On their high holy days, members all prostrate themselves before a giant locust idol made of styrofoam.

THE SHRINE OF JOE PEPITONE

This cult possesses divine proof that the spirit of Joe Pepitone lives in six-year-old Francie Gretzer of Morgantown, West Virginia. Bi-weekly seances are conducted by an Appalachian Poltergeist named Floyd.

GLUB

This spiritual group gets its name from the last word spoken by the prophet Leonard when he was drowned in a vat of rose-water by Satan. Fellow cultists exorcise sin by flogging each other with rutabaga leaves.

KARMA-BY-THE-SEA, CALIFORNIA

Yay! I want to enroll in your club. I enclose $25.00 plus twelve drops of my blood arranged in a semi-circle on a parchment of rotting moleskin. I understand that for every 3 cults I join, I get to form a fourth cult, absolutely free. I may terminate membership at any time after accepting three choices if I dare!

Name_____
REAL Name_____
Address_____
Blood Type_____
Age_____

(Persons under 21 require a letter of consent from parent, living or dead.)

YOU AND YOUR CRYSTAL BALL

by Minerva, the Medium Rare

THIS MONTH: *Gazing At a Departed Loved One*

GETTING AN IMAGE

As in most cases, the first images to appear are hazy and cloud-like. They will gradually transform into a more definite pattern as you concentrate.

Focus your *eyes* on the diffused shapes, your *mind* on the spirit of a departed loved one. You'll sense, subtly at first, his presence about to materialize.

As the shapes take definite form, do not act surprised or shocked if he appears unpresentable. After all, he probably wasn't expecting company!

CORRECTING A FAULTY IMAGE

"Rear projectory" is a common mistake of the novice gazer and can be easily rectified by turning the ball *around*. You're facing the wrong side, dummy!

A "split image" is the result of your concentrating on *two* departed loved ones at the same time. Don't be greedy—remove one of them from your thoughts!

Should you contact *someone else's* Uncle Max by mistake, apologize and the image will leave. Notify your Cosmos Supervisor so you won't be charged for the recall.

COMMON GAZING PROBLEMS

The situation above illustrates a simple case of *bad timing*. The problem is that your Uncle Max is currently appearing in the crystal ball of one of your relatives.

Even *worse* timing! Your Uncle Max has reincarnated as a goat in the mountains of Bulgaria. Don't waste time contacting him—he's even less coherent than before!

Interference is usually caused by a faulty psychic transmitter, jamming by a jealous poltergeist, or cosmic overload (there's a lot of it going around).

**GIVE HIM SUPPORT
FROM THE STARS...**

Give Him A

ZODIAC TRUSS

for His Birthday!

Each one hand-painted with a different sign of the Zodiac by a workman born under that sign. Only $24.95 each (except for Sagittarius, which costs a dollar-sixty more).

Zodiac Products, Ltd.

Available at occult drugstores or wherever fine astrological trusses are sold.

COMING UP

NEXT MONTH:

We decided *not* to tell you!

Anyone with half an ounce of ESP knows already!

ONE HOT SUMMER MORNING

One of the very few bright spots on TV these days are the "Charlie Brown Specials." Since these programs score way up there in the ratings, the networks have been bugging "Peanuts" creator, Charles Schulz, to make "Charlie Brown" into a weekly series. So far, he's resisted because he knows it's impossible to maintain high standards while grinding out a show a week (as Danny Kaye, Jerry Lewis, and a host of others have discovered!). We hope that Mr. Schulz continues to hold out, because if he doesn't, we can just imagine some of the typical mediocre TV formats he might be forced to adopt

IF "PEANUTS" WERE A WEEKLY TV SERIES

ARTIST: JACK RICKARD   WRITER: LOU SILVERSTONE

YOUNG DOCTOR BROWN

PEANUT SQUAD

PEANUTS PLACE

CHARLIE BROWN, ATTORNEY FOR THE DEFENSELESS

THE CHUCK BROWN SHOW

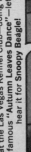

Er-uh—the audience seems to have left, folks! But right over there was sitting Joe Namath! And next to him was Raquel Welch! And over there, Arnold Palmer! And—choke—

Well, that about wraps up tonight's really big shoo, folks! I . . . HUH??

M-my Director informs me that we still have a little time left! Good grief! Forty-five minutes?!?

Well, I guess I'll introduce some of the celebrities in our studio audience . . .

And now, for all you teenagers out there—the comedy impressions of Peppermint Patty! For her first impression . . .

Sorry, Chuck! I refuse to follow an act that refuses to follow an act!

A MAD

LOOK

AT PALM

READING

ARTIST & WRITER: SERGIO ARAGONES

Today everybody seems to be a militant or a protester or some kind of non-conformist. Student radicals, hard-hat construction workers, women's lib fanatics, homosexuals—you name it; they're making themselves heard. MAD, of course, is glad to see all this. Not only does it give these people something to do, it provides us with an excuse to present these

MARCHING SONGS
FOR CRUSADERS, MILITANTS AND ASSORTED, SUNDRY

NON-CONFORMISTS

ARTIST: JACK DAVIS   WRITER: FRANK JACOBS

THE HAWKS' PEP SONG

**(Sung to the tune of
"Bless 'em All")**

Bomb Hanoi!
Bomb Hanoi!
When their troops are too tough to destroy—
A plane-load of bombs from a B-52
Will blast out the rats and the war will be through;
Should you find that the Doves you annoy,
Don't let their complaints mar your joy—
    To hell with the soreheads—
    Use nu-cle-ar warheads
And blow up the world with Hanoi!

THE HYMN OF THE HARD HATS

(Sung to the tune of
"Off We Go, Into The
Wild Blue Yonder!")

Off we go—
In the peace group yonder,
Looking for . . . yippies to chase!
There's a creep—
Tearing our flag asunder!
At him, boys! Step on his face!
C–c–c–crunch!

Raise the flag—
Over this land of freedom!
We'll preserve . . . Liberty's way
   Those filthy Reds
   We'll break their heads
      Yeah
Nothing can stop the Hard Hats today!

THE COLLEGE STUDENTS'
HOMECOMING MARCH

(Sung to the tune of
"When Johnny Comes
Marching Home")

When Johnny comes home from school this year—
    Hoo-hah! Hoo-hah!
The neighbors will know that he is here—
    Hoo-hah! Hoo-hah!
The Vietcong flag from the roof he'll fly
While screaming "Pig!" at each passer-by;
How the block will stare when Johnny comes
    home from school!

When Susie comes home from school this year—
    Hoo-hah! Hoo-hah!
She'll swing like a ten-foot chandelier—
    Hoo-hah! Hoo-hah!
She'll offer grass to her ma and pa;
She'll take the pill and she'll wear no bra;
How the town will buzz when Susie comes home
    from school!

When Freddie comes home from school this year—
   Hoo-hah! Hoo-hah!
His parents will want to disappear—
   Hoo-hah! Hoo-hah!
On Monday morn he'll be marching bare
While quoting Mao in the court-house square,
And we all will know that Freddie's come
   home from school!

When Marvin comes home from school this year—
   Hoo-hah! Hoo-hah!
We won't have a single thing to fear—
   Hoo-hah! Hoo-hah!
He'll wear a crew-cut and mow the grass;
He'll go to church and act middle-class;
   What an awful bore when Marvin comes
home from school!

THE NUDITY-ON-BROADWAY ANTHEM

(Sung to the tune of "On Wisconsin!")

On you actors!
On you actors!
   Play it in the bare!
Shows like "Dolly"
Are more jolly
  When they're done like "Hair"
    (Yeah—Yeah—Yeah!)

Take your shirts off,
Bras and skirts off—
Strip and show your stuff;
We won't stop till we do "Hamlet."
In . . . The . . . buff!

THE COLLEGE RIOTER'S CHANT

(Sung to the tune of *"From the Halls of Montezuma"*)

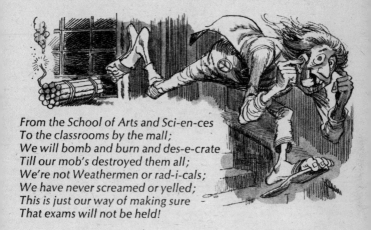

From the School of Arts and Sci-en-ces
To the classrooms by the mall;
We will bomb and burn and des-e-crate
Till our mob's destroyed them all;
We're not Weathermen or rad-i-cals;
We have never screamed or yelled;
This is just our way of making sure
That exams will not be held!

THE WOMEN'S LIB ANTHEM

(Sung to the tune of "The Battle Hymn of the Republic")

Our eyes have seen the glory of the mighty Women's Lib,
When we're free from changing diapers for a baby in a crib;
When we're not enslaved by husbands to a bottle or a bib;
    Our cause is marching on!

(Chorus)

Glory, Glory Hallelujah!
Fight so men will not subdue ya!
If they bitch, then let 'em sue ya!
    Our cause is marching on!

We will crash the clubs for men where women aren't allowed to tread;
We'll go to work as stevedores or lumberjacks instead;
We will fight the Cosa Nostra till the Mob is made co-ed;
    Our cause is marching on!

(Repeat Chorus)

We will shout for Hai Karate when our body sweats and smells;
We will wear the jockey shorts that ev-ry haberdasher sells;
We will work as the attendents in the men's rooms in hotels;
    Our cause is marching on!

(Repeat Chorus)

We will force the Green Bay Packers to allow us on the squad;
We'll elect a woman President, and if you think that's odd…
When we die and go to heaven, we'll elect a woman GOD;
    Our cause is marching on!

(Repeat Chorus)

THE REVOLUTIONARY LEADERS'
ROUSER
(Sung to the tune of
"Over There")

Get your share!
Get your share!
  Write for "Look;"
  Sell a book;
Get your share!
If your words are smutty,
And you look nutty,
You soon will be a millionaire!

Make 'em stare!
Show your flair!
  Be absurd;
  Say "that word"
On the air!
That's the style, man;
Get crude and vile, man;
You'll be (bleeping) rich
  and you'll really

        get your share!

THE POT-SMOKERS' FIGHT SONG

(Sung to the tune of *"Stouthearted Men"*)

Give me some men
Who are pot-smoking men
Who will puff on the stuff they adore;
Making their points
While they're rolling their joints—
On the street, in the park, on the floor—
Oh-h-h-h—

Dizzy and crazy
With heads gettin' hazy,
We're high—through the sky we will soar;
When—
We're all so stoned and bombed that we
    can hardly see—
Then—
Pot-smoking men
Can all flip out on LSD!

THE LONG-HAIR
DRAFTEES' PEP SONG

(Sung to the tune of
"Over Hill, Over Dale")

At Fort Dix
At Fort Knox,
We will hide our bushy locks
As we draftees are keeping our hair;
With a new
Short-hair wig,
They won't toss us in the brig
As we draftees are keeping our hair;
For it's hi-hi-hoo
When a week-end pass comes through—
Let out your hair, Man—don't be square!
We will wear it down
While we all turn on in town—
And we draftees are keeping our hair!

Once

Again

In Front

Of A

Novelty Shop

That's ridiculous! Who's gonna fall for anything as stupid as a Boxing Glove on a lapel? It doesn't make any sense!!
BUS STOP

THE LIGHTER SIDE OF...

BAD HABITS

ARTIST & WRITER: DAVE BERG

Yessiree! I handle things pretty well!

What are you TALKING about?! If you don't have your coffee the minute you get up, you're just no good for the rest of the morning!

And if you don't have a tranquilizer at lunch, you're just no good for the rest of the afternoon! And if you don't have a cocktail before dinner, you're just no good for the rest of the evening!

And if you don't have your sleeping pill before bed, you're just no good for the rest of the night!

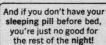

Well . . . other than that, I handle the REST of the day pretty well!

I've got this **really dumb habit!** I'm always **LOSING** things! I've got the largest collection of **"one-of-a-set"** items in captivity —like one glove, one ice skate, one ski pole, and a whole bunch of unmatched one-of-a-kind socks!

Then I found out that **Charlie McGilla** has the **same** dumb habit! He **also** has a huge collection of single items! So I put together a bundle of my single items, and I went over to his house to see if we could **match them up!**

What a **clever idea!** How did it work out?

Not too well!

On the way over . . . I **LOST** the bundle!!

THERE WAS ONCE A TIME WHEN YOU BOUGHT A PRODUCT MARKED "10¢ OFF" ... AND YOU SIMPLY GOT 10¢ OFF! TODAY, ALL THAT HAS CHANGED! TAKE A LOOK...

TODAY, THERE ARE HITCHES, AND CATCHES, AND QUALIFYING STATEMENTS IN SMALL PRINT! TODAY, YOU HAVE TO BE VERY CAREFUL YOU DON'T FALL FOR:

DECEPTIVE MONEY

SAVING
LABELS

PHOTOGRAPHY: BY IRVING SCHILD
WRITER: DICK DE BARTOLO

Cannedwell **SOUP**

SAVE $1.00*!

*WHEN YOU'RE THROUGH WITH THE SOUP, USE THIS EMPTY CAN AS A PIGGY BANK! YOU'LL SAVE OVER ONE DOLLAR IN PENNIES IN IT!

BOGUS BRAND VITAMINS

SAVE 50¢*!

*We'd like to charge you something ridiculous, like . . . $1.50
But the Government will only permit us to charge you $1.00
SO YOU SAVE . . . . 50¢!

BOGUS BRAND VITAMINS

SMALL ECONOMY SIZE

SAVE 85¢*!

FRITZ CRACKERS

*By buying this Small Economy Size and eating all the crackers, rather than buying the Giant Economy Size and letting half of them go stale!

NOSEY-WIPES

Clean Up Stubborn Sneezes

SAVE 6¢*!

*Don't bother to send us the worthless coupon inside the package and save 6c on the stamp!

NOSEY-WIPES

**Head &
Armpits**

shampoo

**BUY
NOW!
SAVE
32¢*!**

*★ ECONOMIC STUDIES INDICATE
THAT THIS BOTTLE OF "HEAD &
ARMPITS" SHAMPOO WILL COST
32¢ MORE IF PRESENT
RATE OF INFLATION CONTINUES!*

GREAT SCOTT! DEPT.

TEN—HUT!! Okay... now hear this, you @#$%¢&! MAD readers, and hear it good! I know you don't usually read any @#$%¢&! introductions to articles in this @#$%¢&! magazine... but you're going to read this one!

And you're going to read this @#$%¢&! introduction because I TOLD you to! And what's more, you're going to read the rest of the @#$%¢&! article that follows this @#$%¢&! introduction, and you're going to read it FIRST!!

You're NOT going to turn to "You Know You're Really A @#$%¢&! When..." or Dave Berg's "The Lighter Side Of @#$%¢&!" You're going to read THIS because it's a @#$%¢&! funny satire of a @#$%¢&! great movie about my @#$%¢&! great life as a chicken-@#$%¢&! General during W.W. II!

Hey, you out there! Stop picking your @#$%¢&! nose and pay attention to me, or I'll kick your @#$ $%¢&! all the way from here to Berlin!

And YOU—you @#¢$%&! cheap little eight-year old @#$%¢&! @#$%¢&! story at the magazine rack and BUY your own copy, or I'll draft your @#$%¢&! right into the @#$%¢&! Army!

Now, here's my military philosophy! No @#$%¢&! ever won a war by dying for his country! You win a war by letting the OTHER @#$%¢&! die for HIS country!

And HOW do you let the OTHER @#$%¢&! die for his country? You KILL the other @#$%¢&! THAT'S how!

So if you want to win a war, you gotta kill every other @#$%¢&! And if that includes ENEMY @#$%¢&!'s— so much the better! All right! You will now sit and pay attention and you will begin reading this story about killing other @#$%¢&!'s... and you will finish it... and you will enjoy it... and that's a @#$%¢&! order! Otherwise, you'll answer to...

PUT✦ON

✦ON

DRUCKER

They don't make wars like they used to! Gee I miss the Spanish Inquisition! The water torture! The cutting out of tongues! Why don't we cut out tongues anymore? And who remembers what's-his-name? Attila The Hun!? What a wild, crazy nut... with his pillage and rapine! What ever became of pillage and rapine!

And what about that Oriental kook, Ghengis Khan, and his lovable Hordes? Gee, I'd love to slaughter with my own Horde! And what about those goofy Crusaders with their torture racks for Pagans—burning heretics in the name of God? What's become of us? Why aren't we religious anymore?

The old man going down Memory Lane again?

Shhh! Don't disturb an old soldier and his dreams!

Brilliant, George! One of the greatest single-handed feats of this war! One of the greatest feats of this century!

You call this a WAR?! You call this a CENTURY!?

BLAM

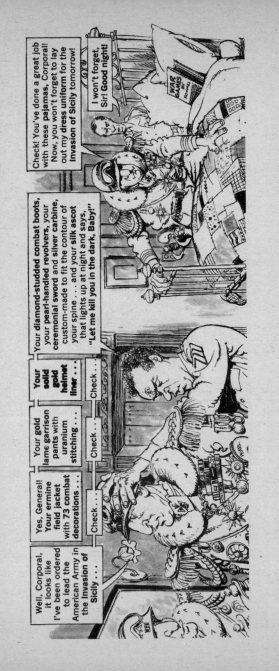

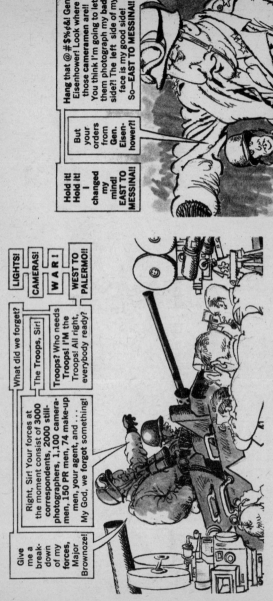

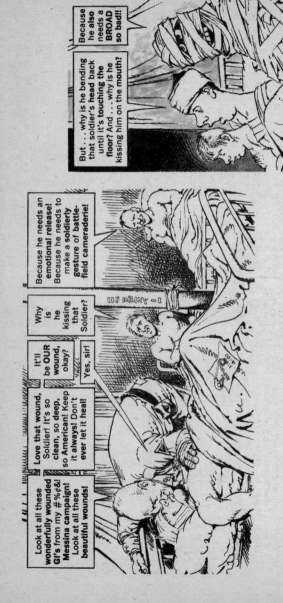